Metal Thread Embroidery

Metal Thread Embroidery

Edna Wark

Kangaroo Press

Other books by Edna Wark:

Drawn Thread Embroidery, Batsford, 1979, re-printed in paperback, 1987
Craft of Patchwork, Batsford, 1984, American edition, 1984, Spanish edition, 1985
Making Fabric Bags, Kangaroo Press, 1985

Acknowledgments

The preparation of this book has been greatly assisted by Susan with a typewriter, Ruth with a camera, Nance with a needle and a pen, Arnold for help with proof reading, and William, ever patient and encouraging. I say 'Thank you'.

I also wish to thank the Embroiderers' Guild in Melbourne and Sydney, as well as various colleagues who allowed me to photograph their work and use their slides.

First published in 1989 by Kangaroo Press Pty Ltd
3 Whitehall Road (P.O. Box 75) Kenthurst 2156
Typeset by G. T. Setters Pty Limited
Printed in Singapore by Kyodo-Shing Loong Printing Industries Pte Ltd

ISBN 0 86417 242 7

Contents

Introduction

Embroidery is a form of textile decoration worked with a threaded needle. The thread which passes through the eye of the needle may vary in many ways. It may be coarse; it may be exceedingly fine. It may be roughly textured; it may be silky smooth. The size of the eye of the needle must be compatible with the coarseness or fineness of the thread for ease of threading. The type of fabric that is available for the background material will have considerable bearing on the kind of embroidery that may be used most happily on it.

Embroidery 'sits' on the surface of the fabric although in most cases the individual stitches pass through the fabric. This statement immediately explains the difference between metal thread embroidery and all other forms of embroidery, except Beading where the basic technique is similar.

Metal threads are made of metal. This seems a simple statement and sounds an obvious one but today with the constant and growing use of synthetics, the viewer with no specialist knowledge makes no recognition of the differences, although the price is usually an indication.

Some people find that working with metal threads is hard on their hands. I cannot say that I have found it so. A few people find that their skin chemistry causes the threads to tarnish while working with them. This makes it inadvisable for them to pursue this area of embroidery.

Lurex, by its cheapness of manufacture, has made the inclusion of 'glitter' in fabrics and trimmings widespread. Lurex can be used in so many ways, and the range of threads has been widened considerably. Placed alongside genuine metal threads, the synthetic ones are usually noticeably different. However this gives us opportunities for greater variety by using the two kinds of thread in combination. Lurex threads can also be used in machine embroidery in a way that most metal threads cannot.

My first introduction to metal thread embroidery came when I arrived in London at the beginning of 1968. I had decided that during my visit, which was to last three years, I would learn all I could about embroidery. It was a subject which had always interested me but, because of family and other commitments, it had only been a peripheral interest. I attended classes at The Royal School of Needlework and The Embroiderers' Guild which introduced me to many fascinating techniques, but it was metal thread work that took hold of my imagination from the very first class.

Here was a technique about which I knew nothing. As I had always lived in a country with no cathedrals with lavish vestments and furnishings, and where State occasions were very simple compared with those in the United Kingdom, the splendour of this technique took my breath away. The possibilities which opened up as I learnt more and more were still expanding nearly 20 years later.

I was led, by lateral thinking, into other crafts, and at one time I explored the techniques of silver work—especially the 'lost wax' process. I came back to embroidery clearly knowing that my embroidery influenced my silver work far more than my silver work influenced my embroidery. It did provide me with a strong and reliable way of attaching 'found objects' to fabric. I have since worked out another technique—an embroidery one—which I prefer in most respects. Both techniques are described in Chapter 12 'Creating Texture with Stitches' under 'Jewels'.

The whole history of metal thread embroidery goes back so far into the past that its origins are lost. Embroidery was in use in China at least three thousand years BC but we do not know precisely when gold thread was introduced. The technique of using wires is not a Chinese one.

In the Bible the use of gold and silver embroidery is mentioned on a number of occasions.

I have watched the threads being made in England and I have found the process fascinating. I have read that the process is basically the same as that used in India centuries ago.

In different parts of the world different areas of the craft have become traditional. Unfortunately I have no knowledge of Eastern languages and have to rely on the research of others. However this does not interfere with my enjoyment and appreciation of the finished objects.

Of course, embroidery worked with metal threads is very expensive. In the last two decades prices of gold and silver have skyrocketed and so anything made with these metals has consequently become more costly. In commissioned work the embroiderer must make sure that the purchaser is aware of the costs involved. Techniques used are very time-consuming and labour has to be paid for too. But there is no doubt that the finished object is very rewarding to the viewer and the executant.

I was never happier than when I had a needle in my hand and a piece of metal thread embroidery under way. My love of this work is almost a reverence, certainly an addiction and I have tried to impart this to others. However I have also tried to deter students from rushing into vast initial purchases of supplies until they found out whether they would want to continue with it.

I have tried to use the medium in traditional ways and in unusual ones. I used them in conjunction with treasures as diverse as chunky stained glass and fragments of natural shell. I have even successfully embedded metal threads in clear plastic as paper weights.

When travelling I was constantly on the watch for new threads or new ways of using them. Friends kept their eyes open and brought me things, and how glad I was! I tried to make articles which were small enough to be within the financial possibilities of my friends, so that this rich and lovely work could be a joy in our everyday life. I also enjoyed making vestments and furnishings for ecclesiastical purposes. These give opportunity for working on a scale that is quite different from the domestic pieces. One must consider how distance emphasises the need for broad impact of design and colour, but close viewing requires refinement of detail and stitch.

I will not attempt to assess or detail ecclesiastical or heraldic embroideries which have been so ably covered by Beryl Dean in her books. She is an artist, a teacher, and an expert practitioner for whom I have a tremendous admiration. My classes with her, which extended my horizons so considerably, would not have been so successful if I had not already absorbed so much from my other tutors in London. To all of them I say a heartfelt 'Thank you'.

Books about music and art relate not only to the techniques but also to the appreciation of these subjects, and my intention with this book is to help travellers and others who visit museums and historical buildings with art collections to appreciate the collections which include historical furnishings and clothing decorated with metal thread embroidery.

In the following pages there are photographs and descriptions of work done in many parts of the world, and for those who wish to go one step further there is a section on techniques.

I have searched far and wide for some of the information in this book. I hope others will read and enjoy my findings and be encouraged to search further themselves. Odd interesting facts do not necessarily come from recognised embroidery books.

E.W., Melbourne, 1989

Hunting pouch of Maximilian I. Courtesy Bayerischesmuseum, Munich. Metal thread embroidery in gold and silver on a pale green velvet background with an ornamented metal clasp and mount.

1. Metal Threads and their Manufacture

Pauline Johnson remarks in her book on Byzantine Church Embroidery: 'the wonderful property of gold is to catch and hold light'. The vestments used in the great cathedrals of Europe were made when the only lighting came from the daylight filtered through stained glass or from candles. A piece of metal thread embroidery looks better if it is not placed in a strong light. A spotlight makes the threads look too shiny; a duller light causes them to glow warmly and as you move around it you can see how the light changes and keeps your interest in it.

Gold and silver threads are made from gold and silver respectively. Gilt threads are made of silver with a coating of gold. The thicker the coating the less the threads will tarnish but it means the cost will be higher. Today gold threads are no longer made; silver threads are made with a core of white metal.

Threads are also made in copper and aluminium. In eastern countries and in France in the seventeenth century, some of the threads were silver or gold on a copper base. In France these were known as false gold or false silver.

It is not possible to tell the quality of the coating of gold just by looking at the threads. It is measured as a percentage of the total weight, e.g. 1 per cent or 2½ per cent.

Gold and silver threads are usually available from the maker or from speciality suppliers, but copper and aluminium are not always available. Manufacturers will usually make special orders for which there will be a minimum quantity that will be an acceptable order. Enquiries must be made to the manufacturer for this information. These threads are all sold by weight.

There are three main varieties of threads:

1. Threads that are laid on the surface of the fabric and couched in place such as Japanese gold and substitutes, passing threads, twists, plate and cords.
2. Purls. These are hollow coils made with very fine wires wound around a spindle. They are then cut into small pieces and the needle and thread goes through each piece as through a bead. All the metal remains on the surface of the fabric. These cut pieces are known as 'chips'. Pearled purl

is a much coarser, stiffer, coiled wire which has been wound around a round spindle and is also couched on the surface of the material.

3. Threads that can be taken through the fabric in the eye of a needle. Passing threads have a core of thread within the casing of fine wire which may be sewn through the fabric. Plate can also be taken backwards and forwards through the fabric provided that the end is shaped to a point.

To make the best use of these threads in all their diversity and brilliance, one must become familiar with their characteristics and their possibilities.

Let us look at these varieties of threads in more detail.

1. Threads for Couching

All sorts of cords and twists can be couched either in separate areas or in conjunction to give contrast and variety. Charles Germaine de St Aubin writing in his eighteenth century publication does not think highly of couched work: 'When the silk threads wear out the metal threads fall off. It is usually used on small articles for sale at fairs'. However large areas of couched gold form backgrounds in many large pieces of work made outside France with the couching in straight or curving lines or even spiralling patterns.

In the earliest metal thread work a fine strip of metal was wound around a core. The core was one hair of a horse's tail, and a horse's hair was used to sew it in place. Later a strand of tightly twisted silk was used but the name 'Horse Tail' continued to be used for the thread. I do not know whether it is still obtainable. It was firm, strong, tightly twisted and came in two shades of yellow and grey.

Young Y. Chung describes the traditional metal thread used in China:

In China gold and silver yarns for metal thread embroidery were made by pounding gold and silver stock into leaf which was then sliced into very narrow strips and then rolled or twisted into yarn. Gold paper or gold painted paper, which was more economical, was also used for this purpose and threads were wrapped in the same way. Such yarns were always couched on the surface of the fabric using a hidden stitch, since stitching through metal threads would have caused the gold and silver to fray and fall off onto the fabric.

Plate is a strip of metal which can be couched on the surface of the fabric. Variation can be introduced by crimping it, which is done by pressing the plate onto the teeth of a comb or the spiral of a large screw. Plate is used in the East far more than in Europe, today.

A nineteenth century development in the making of metal threads was invented by the Japanese. The method was to deposit a coating of gold or silver on rice paper, then to cut it into fine strips and wrap it around a core of silk. This became known as Japanese gold or Japanese silver, frequently shortened to Jap. gold or Jap. silver. It was more reasonably priced than earlier threads. It did have the deficiency that dampness in the atmosphere caused the rice-paper backing to deteriorate.

Plate 1: Angel by Beryl Dean, London, 1982. In 1981 Fr. Nigel Wright of Melbourne sent drawings of three angels to Beryl Dean and commissioned her to embroider a collar for a chasuble using them. He wished her to use a wide variety of stitches including *or nué*. This angel is centre back of the collar. The chasuble is made of handwoven silk.

Plate 4: Jewellery by Jean Goldberg, Melbourne, 1986. Jean uses wires of all kinds to make pieces in needle-lace techniques. These necklets are of stainless steel wire.

Plate 2: Detail of Plate 1, showing example of *or nué* technique.

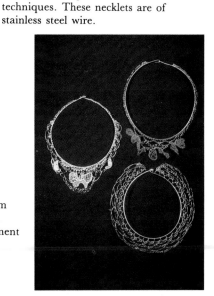

Plate 3: Another angel from the same collar as Plate 1. Note the interesting treatment of the hair.

Plate 5: Details of Chinese border, Ch'ing Dynasty. 20 cm (8 in) by 2 m (6 ft). Gold laid work and silk embroidery on a red silk ground.

Plate 6: Japanese bird, late 18th—early 19th century Silver embroidery on black satin. Small amount of silk embroidery. Detail of a large screen.

Plate 7: Indian bird, probably 19th century. Embroiderers' Guild, Sydney. Silver bullion and silk embroidery on a silvery satin ground.

Plate 8: Indian belt, contemporary, purchased in Agra. Black velvet with gold and silver pearled purl, purls and polished agates.

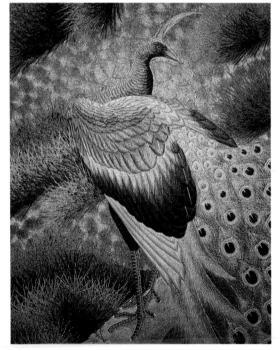

Plate 9: Large Indian panel, late 19th-early 20th century. Very 'pink' gold thread couched in whorls in the background. The remainder of the panel is covered with rich silk embroidery.

15

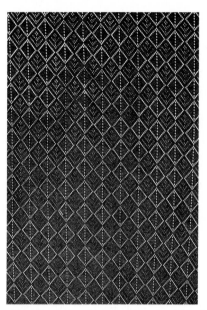

Plate 11: 'King's Head' by Edna Wark, Melbourne, 1971. Laid threads of Jap. gold and a variety of synthetic threads. Gold kid and jewels.

Plate 10: Stole of black net embroidered with gold and silver foil strip. Embroiderers' Guild Collection, Melbourne. This piece is unusual because of the flower in each segment.

Plate 13: 'Theatre Mask' by Edna Wark, Melbourne, 1985. Couched Jap. gold and floss silk embroidery. Black felt cap.

Plate 12: 'Sculptured Head' by Edna Wark, Melbourne, 1982. Aluminium passing thread couched over laid string. Small amount of silk embroidery.

Plate 14: 'Portrait of a Lady' by Ruth Marks, Melbourne, 1986. Couched Jap. gold, some silk embroidery, leather and jewels and feathers.

The Jap. threads were made in a variety of thicknesses. The finer they were, the easier it was to turn corners, and traditionally they were used in pairs. For filling large areas a bricking pattern was used where the stitches in one row were placed immediately above or below the spaces in the previous row.

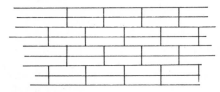

Diagram 1: Bricking pattern for filling in large areas of couching.

Today there is a synthetic Jap. gold and silver which is a strip of Lurex wound around a nylon core. Lurex is a trade name for a process where a very thin film of metal is trapped between two layers of plastic. Although slightly brighter and harsher in appearance than the original Jap. gold and silver, synthetic Jap. gold and silver do not deteriorate with damp. Indeed, when I first received some I soaked it in water to see how it would react. It showed no weakening. Many dress materials containing Lurex threads are washed frequently. Jap. gold or silver is sold in skeins. Substitutes are sold on reels.

With the invention of anodising, which gives the ability to change the surface colour of aluminium, the range of threads has become very colourful.

Aluminium twist and passing thread can usually be obtained from the same suppliers who carry gold and silver stocks.

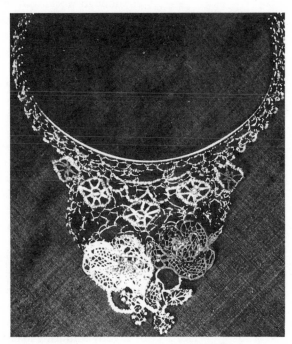

Detail of jewellery by Jean Goldberg, Melbourne, 1988. Stainless steel wire and coloured threads using needle lace techniques.

The fine wires that are used in electronic circuits are sometimes couched onto material, and as they come in colours for coding purposes they can be of interest. Arlene Fish, an American jeweller, uses them for knitting collars and other items. Jean Goldberg of Melbourne uses stainless steel wire for her lace jewellery, examples of which are shown on the previous page and in colour plate 4.

2. Purls

Coloured purls were used extensively in the seventeenth century, particularly in stump work. These were sometimes painted and sometimes they were varnished. Methods of making threads may vary from century to century but the ideas are rarely new.

The name 'purl' derives from an Elizabethan word—'purling' or 'pyrling'—meaning decoration, and is also a lace term. There are two distinct kinds and variety exists in both areas.

When the fine wire is wound around a round spindle the resultant coil looks just like any metal spring, but does not have the ability to return to its original span if stretched. Thus purls should be treated with great care and not be stretched. If this round coil is shiny it is called 'smooth purl'; if it has a satin-like sheen it is called 'rough purl'. Smooth purl is rough purl which has been polished. Rough purl has a mellow, softer appearance than smooth purl which reflects more light.

'Check purls' are obtained when the fine wires are wound around a triangular spindle. They thus have a series of tiny facets which catch and reflect more light than the round ones.

Although working with purls in embroidery is similar to using beads, purls are flexible and can be looped and twisted in a way that beads cannot.

The manufacture of the purls starts with the manufacture of the very fine wires from which they are made. The process starts with a bar of silver about 1 metre (40 inches) long. It is about 4 centimetres (1½ inches) in diameter. Gold leaf is placed on the surface of a wooden table—the thickness of the gold leaf determines the eventual thickness of the gold coating on the wires. The bar of silver is rolled across the gold leaf by hand. The gold adheres to the silver. It is then treated with heat before the process of drawing the wire commences. The wire is drawn through smaller and smaller holes in the drawing plate until that original bar of gold-plated silver has become several hundred (maybe as much as 400) miles of fine wire.

The astonishing thing is that the process has developed by trial and error over the centuries and is still crafted in the same way. Admittedly, the power for stretching the wires is now provided by electricity whereas formerly it would have been powered by horse or man, and the furnaces for heating the metal to make it malleable will be fired by gas or electricity instead of wood. However it is sufficiently a hand-crafted process for every batch of thread to be slightly different.

The wires are then wrapped around fine spindles to make the purls. These wires vary in thickness—there are nine grades in all. The numbering can be slightly confusing to begin with: the coarsest is No. 3, the finest is No. 9.

It seemed to me slightly ludicrous to learn that the makers of these infinitely fine, precious wires belonged to the Guild of the Wire Spinners and Drawers who make Cyclone fencing and similar products.

This description of the process is as I saw it at the factory of Stephen Simpson Ltd, at Preston in England. Chambers Encyclopaedia says that this method of drawing wire has been known since the sixth century BC.

Spangles were made by a different method. Wire was wound around a spindle then the coil was cut into individual links and flattened by beating, leaving a small hole in the middle.

In India the coarsest grade of drawn wire was hammered flat then cut into small pieces with scissors.

In Lappland the tin or pewter thread used is akin to pearled purl, but being made from a much softer metal it must have a thread through the centre to support the coil to prevent it stretching.

Aluminium purls are not made for general sale now. I have some and I like them—they are so much more subtle than silver and do not tarnish badly. But since they required all the same handling in the processing as the silver and gold purls they were little cheaper in the cost analysis than the silver ones, and the market did not take to them. They can be obtained on special order, as far as I know.

3. Stitching with Metal Thread

In Turkey, plate is used to do 'drawn fabric' or 'pulled thread' work. It is also used to do a closely worked all-over pattern on satin. The strip is shaped to a point and taken back and forth through the fabric. Plate is used in the same manner in India where it is usually worked on fine muslins and in some places on cotton net.

These techniques using plate are worked on widely varying fabrics whereas the passing threads require a loosely woven material to make an open lacy pattern.

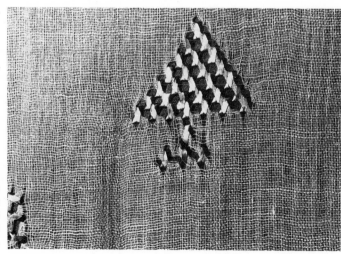

Turkish, 20th century. Detail of a tree on a small tablemat worked in foil strip on green cotton material similar to cheesecloth. Actual size of tree about 2 cm (1 in).

In the days when individual craftsmen made the wires that were necessary for the manufacture of the different metal threads, the one who made the passing thread had to hammer one side of the drawn wire flat so that it would be easier to wrap around the core of thread. At a later date it was passed between rollers which flattened both sides.

Miss Lambert in *Decorative Needlework*, published by John Murray in London in 1843, writes:

> All the wire made in England was manufactured by hand until 1505 when the art of drawing with mills was introduced. Jacob Momma and Daniel Demetrius first established a manufactory for drawing wire at Esher and it is said that the first flatting mill was erected at Sheen near Richmond, in 1663, by a Dutchman, who began to prepare fine gold and silver, such as could be used for spinning around silk for weaving—which before that period had been manufactured only on the Continent...
>
> It is said that the first machine for wire drawing was invented by Rudolph, at Nuremburg in 1360. Antoine Fournier, a Frenchman, brought an improved art of wire drawing to Nuremburg in 1570.

Symonds and Preece in *Needlework Through the Ages* (Hodder & Stoughton, 1928) say that: 'Wire drawing in India is said to have been first practised by the Mohammedans but ancient writings refer to a cruder method long before their conquests'. The method as described by an anonymous writer in the Indian newspaper—the *Oudh Gazette*—in 1870 is of interest. It concludes:

> The process described is identical with that used in Europe; the only difference is that the European workman is supplied with motive power from a perpetual band worked by a steam engine and the native workman uses his marvellously flexible toes for the same purpose.

This note is from *Industrial Arts of India* by George Birdwood, published in India in 1880.

Quoting from Symonds and Preece once again:

> Metal Threads in textile decoration probably owe their importance in the first place to the symbolic significance attached to gold by the ancient sun worshippers. Its brilliance for them had the magical power of the sun... The reputed golden gardens of Peru, with the great life-size beasts and trees in solid gold did not represent vulgar wealth to the sun worshippers of America as they did to their Spanish conquerors any more than did the gift of gold at Bethlehem by the "wise men" from the distant Orient... The early use of gold in Babylonian embroideries may be attributed to the same motive. Passed on to Assyrians and the Persians it also has an aesthetic value in an age of extravagant luxury. Among the splendid spoils of Persepolis were many garments of gold cloth.

The mixture of gold threads in the fabrics apparently did not add to their comfort and this section goes on:

This objection by men to the discomfort of their magnificent woven garments may have had its influence on embroidery with gold and the manner in which the metal was prepared for that purpose, particularly to obtain lightness and flexility . . .

The great ductility of gold permits hammering to any extent . . . From the thin sheet were cut the spangles and the shapes used as a form of appliqué in embroidery common to Babylon, Assyria, Persia, Greece and India: of such, many thousands, beautifully chased, have been found in graves in South Russia and are now in the Hermitage Museum.

2. The Orient

In her very good book *The Art of Oriental Embroidery* Young Y. Chung states that embroidery with silk was done in China 2000 years BC. There had been close ties of trade and politics between China and Korea for centuries. From China embroidery spread to Korea and Japan. Each country in its own time formulated its own style although there were similarities between all three. Young Y. Chung states: 'In colour the Japanese usage leaned to soft, pastel tones, whereas Chinese colour was rich and opulent and Korean colour was bright and vivid.'

One individual characteristic of Chinese work that is noticeable is that usually gold threads are couched with a red silk thread. This gives a warmer tone to the gold.

Symbols were a characteristic element in Chinese embroidery. Badges of rank were an important item on clothing and eventually the dragon became the focal point of the garments at the emperor's court. These dragons signified membership of the emperor's family and entourage. The wonderfully elaborate dragon robes had scarcely any areas that were not covered by intricate, ornate decoration in lavish silk embroidery and much couched gold.

There were subtle differences in the dragons—notably in the number of claws. Five claws denoted the emperor himself. Symbols for longevity, happiness, peace, etc. are to be found in these designs along with symbols for water, land and air.

Before the dragon emblem became the main feature on robes it had made its appearance in much smaller forms on belts. Young Y. Chung says:

> In the main, Chinese work can be typified by its power, symbol-laden content and grandeur of imperial elegance, while Japanese robe embroidery is more delicate, restrained, lyrical, more purely poetic in an artistic sense. Both are certainly equal in quality, both achieved a mastery in the textile arts that is without any precedence in the history of art. But like the Chinese artist, the Japanese embroiderer sought to paint with needles and in painting the design a very special national style emerged.

In Chinese work the ends of couched threads are not taken through the fabric. They are stitched right to the end and another section of the design covers the ends wherever possible. With wrapped threads this is possible but with passing thread the ends unravel very quickly unless the metal thread

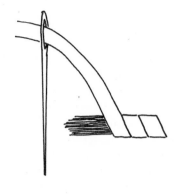
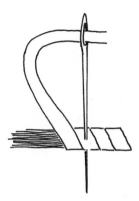

Diagram 2: Preventing passing thread from unravelling.

is unwound from the core for about a centimetre (½ inch) from the end. Thread this metal thread into the eye of a needle and take it through the passing thread just behind the end of the metal thread encasing the core. (See Diag. 2) Passing thread is usually taken through to the back.

Colour plate 5 is of an old piece of Chinese embroidery in a private collection in Melbourne. It is dated as being Ch'ing Dynasty although the style of garments worn by the characters is of an earlier period. The piece is about 2 metres (6 feet) long and about 20 centimetres (8 inches) wide. The background is a dark red satin with a fine gold stripe in some areas.

One fascinating thing for a metal-thread worker in this piece is that the techniques that we use today are still the same as those used in this example. A detail of the skirt panel on one garment shows where the gold has worn away leaving exposed the couched string of the basket weave padding.

The robe of the main character bears the dragon symbol but we cannot see the number of claws. There is an interesting distinction in the embroidery of the faces. For the central character the silk is untwisted, laid vertically, and then the details hold the threads in place. There is the slightest padding under the face. With the other faces a twisted silk has been used in most cases.

The supporting fabric for the satin is a very coarse, stout hessian type of fabric which was the traditional support fabric used in China from the earliest times.

Also included in this embroidery were masses of silk knots. They depict one of the silk embroidered rugs hanging on the wall, and this rug is about 7.5 by 4 centimetres (3 by 1½ inches).

In keeping with the simplicity of furnishings in Japanese homes the style of design which developed was simple, more open than the opulent and rich designs used in the courtly setting of the imperial palaces.

Iwao Saito states in his book on teaching contemporary Japanese embroidery that: 'the Japanese did not have a unique style of embroidery. They have absorbed techniques from elsewhere and refined them to their wishes and requirements...'

Japanese designs make use of beautiful floral motifs using cherry blossom, peach blossom and lotus lilies; and Japanese treatment of birds such as cranes depicts them as elegant and weightless in appearance. Details are added with couched gold or silver thread.

The techniques illustrated in the book by Iwao Saito are similar to those in other publications except for one variation in couching. The usual method is for two threads to be held side by side and when returning the couching stitches are placed in a brick pattern. Iwao Saito gives an example where a single thread is used in the second row and the couching is done over this and the lower of the previous two threads. This gives a denser stitch pattern on the middle thread. If the couching thread is a contrasting colour this would give a deeper colour to the stitches in the middle of the three strands. If a heavier strand was used as the middle thread the effect would be different again. This is just an example of the way that an experienced worker can vary the basic techniques.

Padding is used with great skill and effect in the wings of the birds in the example of Japanese work in Colour plate 6. The fabric of this work is in very bad repair and at some time it has been stuck to a stiff imitation leather, but the embroidery is very interesting. It is probably late eighteenth or early nineteenth century.

A technique developed and used in Japan that is not strictly needlework, but of interest in this context, is the transferring of gold leaf to fabric in stencilled patterns. The stencils are placed on the fabric and a paste applied to the fabric through the voided areas. While the paste is still wet, gold leaf is pressed onto the fabric. When the paste is dry, the gold leaf adheres and where there was no paste, the gold leaf can be removed. With contemporary use of paints, dyes and screen printing as part of embroidery designs, this technique, used in Japan more than 1000 years ago, is not outmoded. It is known as 'Nuihaku' (gold leaf appliqué).

The Indians use a similar technique where they transfer the glued designs with carved wooden blocks.

Nowhere in China, Korea or Japan do the hollow threads—the Purls— appear. Today, they can be bought in Hong Kong but they are an imported commodity. Extraordinarily fine gold and silver Passing Thread can be bought in skeins in Hong Kong. It is of Indian origin and is fine enough to tambour.

There is a common ground of embroidery throughout the world. The same techniques occur and individual stitches are remarkably similar, which is probably not so suprising in that what can be done with a threaded needle is limited. This is why I find metal thread embroidery so much more exciting—it gives an extra dimension to what can be done with that threaded needle.

3. India

Indian metal thread embroidery differs completely from Chinese, Korean and Japanese work. They use the wires in interesting and imaginative ways and by including precious and semiprecious stones, the work assumes great glamour.

When the Greeks arrived in India in the time of Alexander the Great, they noticed that rich garments were worked in gold. That was in 365–323 BC.

Because of the British connection with India there have been many descriptions of embroidered work written in English in memoirs and published reports.

The range of articles made in India is extensive—from small items such as caps and shoes to linings of huge tents used when administrators moved from place to place in former times. To add to the brilliance, the embroideries were often put on to fabrics which already incorporated metal threads in the weaving.

This note is from *Needlework through the Ages* by Rosemary Symonds and Louise Preece:

> A saddle cloth or trapping of Indian work which belonged to Tippoo Sahib was taken to England in 1799. It represented the most ornate gold work

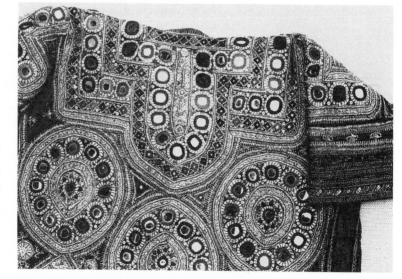

Sind wedding shirt, 20th century. Private collection, Melbourne. The material is a patchwork of coloured fabric pieces with the upper area covered with silver stitching, Shisha glass and coloured embroidery. The decoration is different on the front and back.

of the period and it was of a type known as 'military embroidery' in England. It was highly padded and sculptured in effect. It was carried out in threads, a wide variety of purls, twists, passing threads and pearled purls.

The following report was written in 1888 by T.N. Mukhardj:

Spangles, tinsels, ribbons, thread and wire of silver and gold are made in many of the principal towns, especially those that were seats of government under the Muhammedans. These are used for embroidery and for the decoration on wearing apparel...

...the silver is first made into a round bar tapering at the end, somewhat like a candle and covered with a thin plate of gold. It is called a "Kandlá". The silver ingot then goes to the wire drawer.

By the aid of a simple apparatus he forces the gold plated bar through a series of holes in a stout steel plate, each succeeding hole being narrower and finer than the one before, so that when the Kandlá has passed through the last hole it is reduced to the thinness of an ordinary fine wire.

The wire now goes to the fine wire drawer who draws the wires still more finely by a still more simple apparatus—the wire being fastened to a wheel which is turned by a winch.

The fine wire now goes to the "Dabka" who flattens it out for ribbons and lace making. The flattening is done by hammering.

During the rule of the Mohammedan Court at Burhanpur, in the central provinces, rules were strictly adhered to and quality of threads was tightly controlled. During British rule in India these controls were relaxed. Irwin & Hall tells us that:

...in the 18th century two distinct types of gold embroidery predominated in India—Zardoshi work, heavy gold laid work upon a ground of velvet or satin; and Kalabatan work, light delicate embroidery in gold and silver thread, wire and spangles upon fine silk, cotton or muslin.

The technique of gold embroidery upon velvet is reported to have been introduced into India by the Portuguese. The gold threads are laid over a pre-worked foundation padding of cotton threads, a laborious process which tends to produce a formal style of design. It is particularly suited to ornate saddle cloths, large hangings and floor coverings but perhaps the most impressive pieces of Zardoshi work are elephant trappings, as in older pictures of the state elephants of Jaipur.

By the late nineteenth century a cheaper but superficially effective class of work was made substituting a padding of paper pulp for threads, and the threads had a core of orange cotton, not yellow silk.

In 1880 George M. Birdwood wrote a book on the *Industrial Arts of India* which was republished in 1974. He writes:

There is no doubt that the brocades of Ahmadabad and Benares and Murshedabad represent the rich stuffs of Babylon, wrought as we know they were with figures of animals in gold and variegated colours. Such brocades are now a speciality of Benares.

Pair of Indian slippers. Private collection, Melbourne. Pink velvet embroidered in silver thread and spangles.

Fine weaving probably passed from India to Assyria to Egypt and then through the Phoenicians into southern Europe: and gold was in-woven with cotton in India, Egypt, Chaldea, Assyria, Babylon and Phoenicia from the earliest times...

In Psalm XLV—Upon the right-hand did stand the Queen in gold of Ophir...the king's daughter is all glorious within: her raiment is of wrought gold.

J.B. Fuller in his report to the Indian government says:

Gold and silver wires are often introduced in the manufacture of the more valuable fabrics.

The metal threads may be used only in the borders or patterns or they may be used so lavishly that the whole fabric appears to be made of gold or silver.

There were many centres where these beautiful fabrics were made and embroideries done but Benares in northern India has always been an important source. Lucknow has also been an important centre for work done on fine muslin and in Madras the wires and beetle wings were used on net.

Another Indian writer, D.P. Taraporevala, says:

Lucknow has also been known for another kind of embroidery called Badla. This is done with a flat metal thread that serves as a needle itself and is taken in and out of the material and pressed into the required motifs.

There is a child's frock in the collection at the Power House Museum in Sydney said to be Indian. It is silver on white net and the technique Taraporevala describes has been used.

Of Indian textile designs Taraporevala writes:

The charm of their textile fabrics lies in the simplicity and treatment of the decorative details... The objects are always represented quite flat as in mosaics and generally symmetrically and in alternation.

If you get them to copy a plant, they will peg it down flat on the ground, laying its leaves, buds and flowers out symmetrically on either side of the centre stem, and then only, will they begin to copy it. If the leaves and flowers of the plant are not naturally opposite, but alternate, they will add to them others to make it so.

Three is a usual element in Indian design: three leaves on a stem, three prongs on a tendril. Palmettes are often introduced and an eight-petalled lotus flower.

The much used pattern which became known through paisley shawls as the paisley pattern was introduced from India where various origins have been attributed to it. Birdwood says it is derived from the lotus bud, Enakshi Bhavnani that it is sometimes referred to as the mango or almond design. I possess a pine cone cut in half and I am inclined to adhere to the name 'cone pattern'.

Much embroidery is still done in India, not only for home use but also for the export and tourist trade. It varies greatly in quality but is still fascinating. The belt in colour plate 8 I bought in Agra—the beads incorporated are agates.

The hanging shown in colour plate 9, the peacock with the gold whorl pattern in the background, is very large. The remainder is completely covered with beautiful silk embroidery. The couched gold is not the predominating feature.

4. The Mediterranean

In earliest times embroidery was not considered a poor relation to art as it was to become in the nineteenth century.

One early Greek poet named Theodore Prodomus in his writings complained of his meagre earnings and how much better off he would have been if he had trained as an embroiderer. This is quoted in notes on Greek handcrafts published by the Bank of Greece.

Ita Aber says that through the ages Jewish society considered 'needlework to be a fine art as well as a personal expression of skill'.

Goldsmithing and silversmithing have been trades notably associated with Jewish craftsmen for centuries. It was these craftsmen who made the metal threads until the Middle Ages. Village craftsmen in India were still making them much later.

When the Jews started leaving their homeland they went in two directions—northwards into Persia, Turkey, the Balkans and Russia, and westwards along the shores of the Mediterranean to Morocco and then into Spain and southern Europe. Later they were driven out of Spain and some went back into Morocco and some into Europe.

In Yemen the Jewish embroiderers worked a distinctive kind of embroidery using a coloured thread to couch gold thread in whorls. The couching of gold thread in whorls was also done in India and southern Germany at times.

The very elaborate metal thread embroidery on costumes worn in the Mediterranean was very definitely an indication of the wealth of the family. On bridal costumes not only metal threads, braids and laces made of wires were used, but coins that were part of the bride's dowry as well.

At its extreme the Moslem bride in the coastal areas of northern Africa wore seven layers of gold-embroidered garments which were very stiff and uncomfortable.

Caroline Stone has published an excellent book on the embroideries of North Africa. She mentions the embroidery done with a metal strip known as 'tal'. It is used as a panel on the front of men's shirts. This type of work is called 'Barmagli'.

In Turkey this kind of embroidery is known as *Tel Kirma*—folded metal.

Examples of work using this narrow metal strip seem to have been done over a wide area. It is mentioned in India, Turkey, Syria and Egypt. It surfaces in Australia from time to time and is probably traceable to travellers coming to Australia by ships which called at Port Said and Bombay, not to mention the many soldiers who served in Egypt in World War I who returned with presents—see colour plate 10.

In the collection of textiles at the University of Washington at Seattle in the United States there is a caftan-type robe which would fit a very large man. It is said to be from the Sudan. It is black net with silver strip embroidery.

Also in the collection at Seattle is an unusual example worked with a metal strip. It is a piece resembling heavy lace. Here the strip has been wound around a cord and a design made with this coarse thread. Ita Aber in her book on Judaic embroidery has an illustration of a similar piece and calls it 'Spanish work'. No one seems to know how the techique is done but it appears to be stitched through the edge with a needle and thread which makes an outline like a buttonhole stitch. No doubt this is the stitching which holds the loops etc. in place. My note on this piece says that the medallions are done alternately in a smooth and a textured strip. This kind of work was much favoured as a collar on a prayer shawl in the Jewish communities.

In the Top Kapi Palace museum in Istanbul there are two interesting examples of embroidery using the metal strip. One is a towel with a wide border including silk flowers but the background of the border is open-work in silver. It has the appearance of four-sided stitch.

The other example is on a gauze drape around the hips of an elaborate woman's court costume. Here the strip over-casts the edge and outlines large eyelets.

In Turkey the women of the harem made many of the household items required for the sultan's palace. Not only were there garments and furnishings to be embroidered but the lovely ceremonial towels with floral borders that were used on formal occasions and given as presents to important visitors. Very important guests such as ambassadors would receive embroidered caftans. These would have been professionally made in well-organised workshops.

'Spanish work'. Textile Collection of Washington University, Seattle. This type of embroidery was a speciality of Jewish workers in Spain and later in Italy.

Greek waistcoat, early 20th century. Presented to the National Gallery of
Victoria by Mrs M. Singer, 1978. D 107/1978. Pale green wool embroidered
with gold couched thread, lined with cream cotton. Note the charming Turk's
cap buttons as ornaments on the edges.

The women in the far eastern area of Turkey known as Georgia were
particularly adept with the needle. They embroidered on finest muslin and
gauze with a fine strip of metal. They embroidered on Morocco leather for
saddles and belts and pouches without spoiling the gold-coated passing
threads.

The Turkish gold-embroidered saddles became prized trophies of war
and were coveted by Europeans as far north as the Baltic states.

The sleeveless Turkish jacket, similar to the bolero, became part of the
national costume in the Balkan states that were overrun by the Turks. They

31

were closely embroidered in laid metal threads. The Greek one illustrated on the previous page is in the collection of the National Gallery in Melbourne.

In Turkey and in Greece the great centres of embroidery were situated around the centres famous for their woven fabrics. Brusa and Joaninna were such centres. The embroiderers could use the threads of silk or metal that were unsuitable for the weavers or in excess of what was needed.

Political events controlled the spread of techniques at times. One such is the Greek technique known as 'chryssonima' where a gold thread is wrapped around a coloured core. The thread was couched as in other countries or it was sometimes more loosely wound so that the coloured core became visible thus giving a different appearance to the gold. The thread was fine and subtle effects were achieved.

This technique was never used in Europe. The period when it was popular in Greece was in the fifteenth century and the sixteenth century when the Turkish expansion in the Balkans had sealed off commercial intercourse with Europe.

Conversely *or nué* reached its highest point in the fourteenth and fifteenth centuries in the workshops in Burgundy (an area which is now part of Belgium) and never became a practised technique in Greece or Turkey.

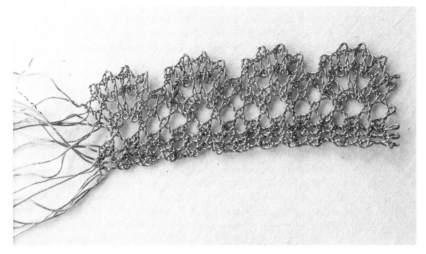

Plate 15: Sample of bobbin lace by Margaret Cardinaletti, Melbourne, 1988. Worked in gilt passing thread which Margaret found did not work easily.

Plate 16: Jewellery by Edna Wark, Melbourne, 1985. Selection includes needleweaving using fine gold threads set in liquid embedding plastic. Coloured purls were used with a baroque cultured pearl. Gold chips were massed around a piece of Trochus shell. One piece shows the back of a piece of work in progress. The detached buttonhole cradle is clearly visible.

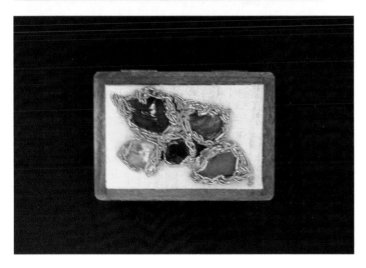

Plate 17: Box with chunks of glass by Edna Wark, Melbourne, 1976. Pieces of chunky coloured glass are held in place with settings and decorated with gold purls.

Plate 18: 'Hot Copper' by Edna Wark, Melbourne, 1971. Silks of many shades have been used to couch synthetic passing threads to reproduce the effect of extreme heat on pieces of copper.

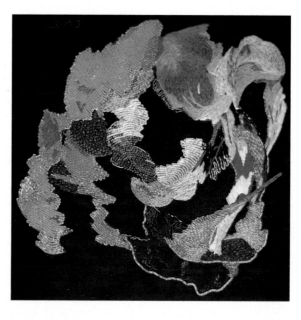

Plate 19: 'St Stephen' by Morna Sturrock, Melbourne, 1974. Worked as a demonstration piece, this small embroidery has the background worked in underside couching.

Plate 20: Design for a burse, a flat cloth case used for carrying the corporal in the celebration of the Eucharist, by Elizabeth Elvin, London, 1982. The wealth of stitch details in this piece repays close study.

Plate 21: Coin purse from Afghanistan, 20th century. Private collection, Sydney. Silver passing thread has been laid over a pattern delineated with string.

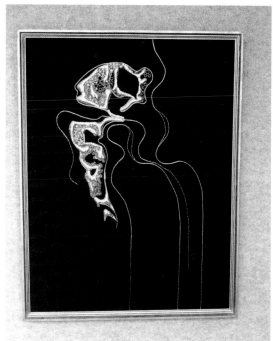

Plate 22: 'Towards Gold' by Lesley Uren, Melbourne, 1985. The design of this 25th anniversary gift grew out of freely placed pieces of gold kid, beautifully applied.

Plate 23: Wedding canopy by Joan Koslan Schwartz, USA, 1976. The back panel of carefully applied Hebrew lettering in gold kid spells out the marriage contract. Pomegranates are embroidered in coloured silks and gold threads.

5. Europe

In France, Italy and Austria the Christian church commissioned elaborate vestments and furnishings, and cathedrals and palaces have collections in their establishments.

There were outstanding workshops in Palermo, Sicily; in Lyons, France, where there was also a large industry making luxury fabrics; in Germany, where the use of corals, pearls and coloured glass beads with metal plates achieved bright coloured effects, and where in the sixteenth century, they made great use of metal threads couched in whorls in backgrounds; in Sweden, where Albert the Embroiderer was famous; and in Burgundy (now a part of Belgium) where the technique known as 'or nué' was developed and perfected. A beautiful example appears on the next page.

In the Victoria and Albert Museum, in London, are two pieces which survive from a set of vestments attributed to the Palermo workshops. One is a collar. The design is in coral beads and the background completely covered with silver bullion embroidery. In the Top Kapi Palace museum in Istanbul there is a prayer mat that bears striking resemblance in its technique to this item. It is also coral beads on a silver bullion background.

In the twelfth and thirteenth centuries very rich ecclesiastical vestments were made in England and found their way into the treasuries of cathedrals and palaces in Europe. They are known as 'Opus Anglicanum'—a much more impressive name than today's equivalent: 'Made in England'.

In Reykjavik in Iceland there are vestments that resemble those made in England at that period. Gertie Wandl, that great lady of Danish embroidery of the twentieth century, told me of these vestments when I visited her about ten years ago. Nothing is known of their history.

In England many of these vestments and furnishings were plundered and dispersed during the Reformation.

Another great period blossomed during the reign of Elizabeth I.

This embroidery was so rich that it has to be seen to be believed. (Look at the photograph on page 39.) We know that in our own time the cost of anything crafted in gold or silver is extremely high. We do not need to know the exact scale of comparison to realise that this form of decoration was always expensive.

The threads were made by craftsmen and so would have had individual differences.

The fine wires, twists, cords, strips and spangles had been used for centuries, but now the hollow threads (the bullions) appear in great quantities

Detail of the Marienmantel in the Kunsthistorisches Museum, Vienna. Worked
in the Burgundian Workshops in the mid-15th century. It is part of a set of
High Mass vestments made for the Order of the Golden Fleece. The entire set
is worked in the technique known as *or nué*.

and with tremendous effect. Remember that with natural lighting or candles
they would have appeared more mellow than under modern lighting.

The purls were used on garments, on furnishings, on palls and on crowns
of livery companies. This is a time when comforts that were previously
unknown were appearing in the great houses. Heavy, solid wooden furniture
was becoming more comfortable with the addition of cushions. Many of
these were embroidered—some with tent-stitch and cross-stitch on canvas
using wool or silk, or using both with touches of gold and silver; but the
most elaborate were velvet cushions ornately embroidered in gold and silver,
and with applied cloth of gold. An interesting point to note in those that
survive, and there are many survivors in collections in the United Kingdom
and some in the United States, is that although the pile of the velvet has
worn away with use the bullion embroidery remains. I have heard it
suggested that the bullion embroidery was to protect the valuable material
so they must have been very costly fabrics.

Beds were important items in the household furnishings and their

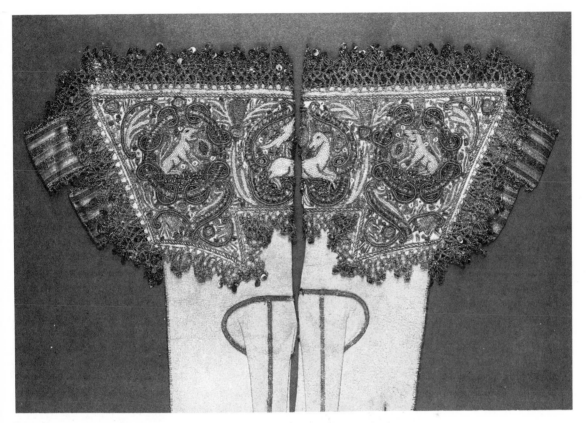

Pair of gloves, late 16th century—early 17th century. Coutesy Museum of Fine Arts, Boston. Gift of Philip Lehman. Leather embroidered with silk, gilt, silver yarns and seed pearls. Accession Number 38,1351 a,b.

decoration was elaborate. A bed with a canopy and curtains was essential. The curtains were drawn for warmth as well as privacy.

There was a valance at the top of the bed to hide the poles from which the curtains hung, then there were the curtains; there was an embroidered band that hid the gap between the mattress support and the floor, not to mention the coverlet and pillow covers. All were embroidered in a planned design.

There is a magnificent state bed at Knole, a stately home in Kent. It is velvet covered with bullion embroidery. The weight of the coverlet alone must be very great.

Curtains were also important to cover windows and doorways. Glazing of windows was a very new and expensive part of construction and rooms opened into each other rather than, as in the later style, into passages and corridors. These made rooms less draughty. In the Isabella Stewart Gardner Museum at Boston, Massachusetts, is a different method of draught control. This museum is built as a replica of an Italian palace. It is a charming five-storey building with a 'light well' above an enclosed courtyard. When I saw it, it was full of spring flowers in tubs. In one of the salons is a huge open fireplace. On either side of the fireplace are hinged brass rods from which are suspended large velvet curtains embroidered with the crest of a German prince who became a Cardinal. They are worked in gold bullion. He lived in the fifteenth century.

The furnishings are authentic pieces brought from Europe in the nineteenth century to furnish this palace which was Mrs Gardner's home.

My imagination falters when I think of the weight of the garments which were worn by people in medieval times. There were many layers, and the velvets and brocades were heavy even before all that metal thread embroidery was set upon sleeves, bodices, skirts, etc.

Much of this embroidery was worked within the great houses. The mistress of the house, her family and household staff all took part in the projects. If they did not have a resident member who drew their designs for them, then a travelling tradesman might do them, or a tutor, or a local artist. George Wingfield Digby in *Elizabethan Embroidery* writes: 'if the furnishings contained large areas of couched gold work they were made by professionals but the ladies of the period were quite used to embroidering with purls'.

At this time in history there were many avenues of trade that were

Drawstring bag, late 16th—early 17th century, English. Gift of Philip Lehman. Courtesy of Fine Arts Museum, Boston. Silk embroidered with silver yarn and wire. Note the decorated tassles. Accession Number 38,1229.

expanding. The sea route to India had been opened up by the Portuguese navigator Vasco da Gama. This made access easier to fabrics and artifacts of India. (When visiting Venice I was told that two major trading houses closed their doors the day the news of Vasco da Gama's successful rounding of the Cape of Good Hope reached them. They realised that their role in the forward distribution of cargoes which had previously come overland and across the Mediterranean could be wiped out.)

Styles of embroidery varied between England and Scotland where Mary Queen of Scots' influence was closer to French styles of fashion and furnishings. The French used some different methods of manufacture in some of their threads. Instead of silver gilt they used a base of copper. These were known as 'false gold' or 'false silver'. A French silversmith, working at the Ottoman Court in Constantinople in the seventeenth century introduced this procedure to the Turks. Wires and strip made by this process are not as brittle as those made on a silver base.

However the threads were still a luxury item, and from time to time governments placed bans on their use to try to force people to economise on the cost of their clothing.

A peculiar custom developed at the French court where ladies would try to remove the bullion decoration from the elaborate coats of the gentlemen. This was known as *parfilage* or 'drizzling'. There were special small scissors and knives made for the purpose which would fit into a lady's purse. The trophies thus obtained would be recycled.

It has been a standard practice through the ages for ceremonial and ecclesiastical robes and furnishings, when worn out or outmoded, to be burnt. The metal was retrieved and recycled.

I remember a friend buying an expensive sari in India just before World War II, and the merchant told her that if she returned it at some later time he would buy it from her for the value of the gold in it.

Regulations differed in various countries but in England in the Middle Ages the apprenticeship for an embroiderer was seven years. It was a man's occupation. The Guilds which controlled the standards of training etc. in Turkey at the same period are well documented.

In biblical times the makers of garments and furnishings for the synagogue were all male. The men were also the professional needleworkers in India. Here they had a distinctive practice of putting the needle into the fabric pointing away from the body. This method is still used in India today.

A few names of famous embroiderers who were women are known to us. Mary Queen of Scots is one of the most famous, and her contemporary, Bess of Hardwick, whose fourth husband was the Earl of Shrewsbury, under whose surveillance Mary lived at one time, is another. Queen Elizabeth I was also an accomplished embroiderer

A.L. Kendrick, in his book *English Needlework*, gives the names of a number of Saxon women whose skills have been recorded.

Sister Agatha is the name of a Byzantine nun whose signed work survives. There is a small panel called 'St George and the Dragon' in the Benaki Museum in Athens that is her work. There are also records of other Byzantine women who were professional embroiderers.

The Huguenots brought to England skills that had been in use in Europe but were new to England. The summer of 1985 edition of *Embroidery* had an article on the origin of the firm founded by a Huguenot in 1685. This firm, run by descendants of the original Toyé family, is still in business and embroidering in metal threads.

French coat, early 19th century. Courtesy Museum of Fine Arts, Boston. Elizabeth Day McCormick Collection. Black broadcloth, gold embroidery. Accession Number 44,273.

When Charles Germain de St Aubin wrote his report in 1770 he was in no doubt as to where the best embroideries were made. I quote:

We French who pay the most thoughtful attention to whatever we do with luxuries have surprisingly benefited from the discoveries of other nations by changing, improving and adapting them in the best manner to new uses. To be convinced of this it suffices to see the masterpieces in the wardrobe of the King and the number of foreigners seeking to obtain our embroidery. They are apparently captivated by the novelty of the materials, the variety of the designs and the beauty of the execution. For great occasions they prefer our products to the sparkle or delicacy of their own.

It was not only court dress at which the French excelled; their ecclesiastical embroideries were also highly regarded.

On the subject of design St Aubin is worth quoting:

I would not be a Designer if I did not maintain (and it would not be difficult for me to prove) that Design is the base and foundation of Embroidery. It provides harmony, regulates the proportions and brings additional merit to the work by the economy of the different materials and the opposition or the blending of diverse methods.

6. Russia and the Baltic States

There is a recently published translation of a Russian book on lace and embroidery, which is kept in the Historical Museum in Moscow. It is fully illustrated—much of it in colour—and gives evidence of a very high standard in the workrooms associated with the noble establishments in Russia in the Middle Ages.

One particular illustration is of a shroud or pall made in the sewing rooms of Princess Staritsky in the 1560s. There is a central medallion surrounded by 12 smaller ones. The variety of couched patterns in the garments is outstanding.

A number of women's hats are illustrated. Some are rich in embroidery and seed pearls, some in gold embroidery.

Another illustration in the book has a raised design which gives an impression similar to relief metal work. The notes say the motifs were made separately and applied and were worked on birch bark or stiff paper. The only other reference I have found to craftsmen working on birch bark is to the beadwork of the North American Indians.

Many spangles of gold and silver were scattered on the background

Detail of mitre, Russian, 19th century. From a distance it appears to be engraved silver. Embroidered in silver thread, seed pearls and jewels and with painted medallions. It is in the National and Ethnological Museum, Athens.

material around and between the scrolling motifs in the manner seen in work of Elizabethan England.

It is remarkable how similar designs were used in widely separated countries. It is a reminder to us that ideas and designs do not need aeroplanes to be exchanged internationally.

During the sixteenth, seventeenth and eighteenth centuries the work was made for ecclesiastical and court use. The styles of design and the quality

Two small panels, dated 1518, from Nuremburg. Courtesy of the Bayerischesmuseum, Munich. Each panel contains a figure in high relief. The garments are of gold and silver with the cloaks and background details in seed pearls. The female figure is Saint Agatha.

of techniques were similar to and equal to anything seen in Europe. In addition to the metal threads and silk embroidery, great use was made of seed pearls. I remember someone who had seen embroideries in Moscow saying to me, 'They used seed pearls like French knots'. This was also a characteristic of work done in southern Germany—see the example on the previous page. It was also a favourite form of embroidery done by Jewish workers. Usually it was a case of using locally obtained supplies.

Decorative towels were made for gifts and were also used on formal occasions. They differed in design and shape to those commonly associated with Turkey. It was customary, in Russia, for the bride to give to every member of the bridegroom's family an embroidered towel. This meant, sometimes, that the bride and her family made and embroidered as many as 100 towels. The eligibility of a young girl was seriously assessed on her ability to embroider and sew.

Bridal sheets were very elaborately embroidered and could have metal thread lace as well. Bobbin laces were made with metal threads and appear on church and household items.

As well as these articles of great worth and lavish production, gold work also appeared on folk costumes and was a gauge of the wealth and standing of the family.

In Russia gold work had practically died out by the end of the nineteenth century and the standard of it had declined generally.

Much beautiful embroidery has been done for centuries by the women of Georgia. One form is done on net with a strip of metal. These strips are narrow and flexible and it is usually done with a pointed end—no needle is used to take it back and forth through the net. This form of embroidery is also done in isolated areas and on the Mediterranean coast of Egypt where

Cap purchased in India. Private collection, Melbourne. Gold embroidery on velvet, probably made in Bukhara.

there have been Georgian immigrants for centuries, be they women in harems or men slaves.

Nearby, but not part of Russia, was an important area where gold embroidery was done. There were well-established workshops in Samarkand and Bukhara by the sixteenth century. The embroidery was all done by men though many of them taught their wives and daughters to do it. The women's names never appeared in the records; they were recorded as so-and-so's wife or daughter.

The work from Bukhara was done on velvet, chamois or woollen material—rarely on silk. The threads were obtained from Russia and India. A trade in gold embroidered caps still flourishes in Bukhara with a market in surrounding countries and as far as India.

Latvia

A difference in style of dress and the decoration on it is often a guide to the status and wealth in folk costume and that was so in Latvia. In the eighteenth century great changes were apparent especially in the northern and central parts.

Aprons in green woollen material decorated with red bands and gilt threads were often worn. The materials were purchased rather than produced at home.

In *Estonian Folk Costume* by Melaine Karma and Aino Voolma, there is an illustration of a detail of embroidery containing coiled bronze wire which has been cut into pieces and applied to the material. The manner in which the pieces are applied appears similar to the accepted use of purls.

They also note the use of spangles of the kind where the metal disc has a tiny snick in the edge where the spangle was held on a jig while the hole was drilled.

Coarse laces in metal thread that appear in illustrations resemble crochet in filet patterns.

Lappland

The Lapps lived in a harsh environment that did not encourage people to stay in one place and build up settled communities. Therefore their crafts were those that they could take with them from place to place. Thus they would tend to be things of personal adornment or use made from supplies that were readily to hand. As they were nomadic herdsmen, furs and hides would be available, also antlers. Somewhere through the centuries someone—a little more imaginative than his forebears—decided to wrap a wire of tin around an animal sinew, and he then had a thread which could be attached with a sinew to a rough woollen garment or one of leather...and so began another craft.

Because the tin wire is very soft it must have a thread through the centre. It is always used as it comes. Traditionally it is not used in any other way.

Lapp tin embroidery, 20th century. Tuula
Marjonien, Sweden. Handbag of reindeer skin with
insert of tin embroidery.

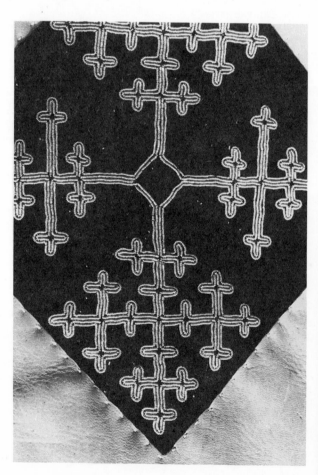

Detail of embroidery on reindeer
skin handbag above.

It is laid in simple geometric patterns on woollen fabric akin to a fine flannel. The colours of this material were black, red or green.

The geometric patterns and the style of pictograms are similar to those of the Eskimos of North America. Some are also similar to Celtic plaited designs. This type of design appears frequently on their carvings on reindeer horn.

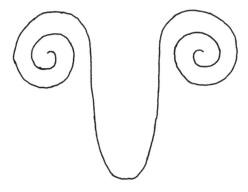

Diagram 3: Pictogram common to many cultures representing a reindeer.

Collars, cuffs and bonnets with tin-thread embroidery are frequently added to everyday clothing for festive occasions.

A Swedish girl named Tuula Marjonien visited Melbourne in 1984. She came to the Embroiderers' Guild where a small group had lessons from her in Lapp tin embroidery. We were interested in her work and the articles that she had to show. The tin embroidery was combined with reindeer skin in bags of various sizes and smaller items such as watch bands and key rings—they were all attractive and useful. The reindeer leather was very tough but pliable.

Tuula showed us one variation on the simple couching of the thread. Two threads could be twisted together to look like a cord when couched.

The museum notes from the Silver Museum at Arjeplog say this:

It was towards the end of the Middle Ages that the Lapps wandered into the markets of the neighbouring Norway with their furs and other wares where they exchanged them for the silver ornaments worn and displayed by Norwegian and German merchants. The mediaeval silver-work was most popular with the Lapps so, therefore, the silversmiths who came later continued to make in this style. Later the nomadic Lapps found their way to the Swedish coast where they had the local craftsmen copy their spoons made of reindeer horn and their plaited figures and flower designs from their wooden pails copied.

The Lapp tin threads were made from tin obtained from England and Ireland. The method used to make a fine thread was as follows: a peg of mountain ash wood was hollowed out by removing the pith. A piece of tin was cast in this and then a thread was spun at a fine tension. To achieve this fine thread it would be drawn through holes in a plate made of reindeer horn called a "wortel".

7. Faces

Faces worked in metal threads have always fascinated me. They appear in many medieval embroideries and there are different ways of doing them.

Early faces made use of whorls to indicate the moulding of cheekbones and chin and later rows fitted in around them.

Here are photographs and notes of several different ways faces can be done. Suffice it to say that the endeavour is to give the impression of modelling using a flat surface.

King's Head, 1971 (Colour plate 11). This was done under instruction from Elizabeth Elvin at the Royal School of Needlework in London.

The Jap. gold thread follows the line of the eyebrows and down the nose as a beginning. If there is a slight downward bend in the rows in the centre of the brow it helps to give an impression of moulding.

In the face the rows are horizontal across the cheeks, and those that make up the eye sockets are rounded. The eyebrows and shadows are indicated by using brown thread to couch the gold. The eyes and mouth were voided. An almost straight line to the lower lid of the eye gives an impression that the face is faintly smiling.

The hair and the beard are worked in various synthetic threads and some pearled purl to give contrast. The crown is gold kid with 'jewels'.

Sculptured Head, 1982 (Colour plate 12). This was embroidered after seeing a picture of a painting in a college chapel in Africa. The painting is on a section of the ceiling. The idea of a face in a square on one corner intrigued me.

String was laid in areas outside the face to simulate locks of hair and a beard. The aluminium passing thread was laid in parallel lines from edge to edge of the background. Whenever the thread reached a ridge of string a stitch was made close to the string, on either side of it. Then if the spaces between the lines of string were wide enough stitches were placed there until another ridge was reached. The stitches on either side of the string were of a darker shade of grey than those used in between or in the face.

In the main the stitching in the face was simple bricking. Exceptions were the brows, the eyes and mouth. The nose gave quite a lot of trouble and had to be strengthened several times.

I commenced the couching at the widest point and worked upwards and then downwards to prevent excessive distortion in the horizontal lines.

Theatre Mask, 1986 (Colour plate 13). This idea came from an oriental illustration.

The initial lines couched were the eyebrows and down the nose. The eye sockets were rounded and the eyes were closely stitched in white and black with grey at the corners.

Creases and shadows were indicated in brown using the *or nué* technique of opening or closing the stitch pattern to give depth of tone. Yellow stitching left highlights gold.

The teeth were worked in cream floss silk and the moustache and beard in black floss silk.

Portrait of a Lady, 1986, Ruth Marks, Melbourne (Colour plate 14). The subject was suggested by a portrait by P.P. Rubens called 'Le Chapeau de Paille'. Ruth commenced with the brow and the nose. Jap. gold is couched in whorls on the cheeks and the chin. The neck area is couched in a perpendicular direction which gives a different reflection of light to the horizontal and circular couching in the face. The basket-stitch around the neckline of the dress is worked over bugle beads. This is a very satisfactory way of doing basket-stitch if the correct length of bead is obtainable. There are no rough ends of string to hide.

See colour plates on page 16.

8. Laces

Laces using gold thread are very old indeed. Network existed in biblical times and elaborate forms of it dating back to 1000 BC have been found in Egypt in tombs. The earliest forms are of linen net darned with gold threads or of examples where net and embroidery are both of gold. Examples were also found in Scandinavian graves in Dorset in England with twisting and plaiting of gold threads. See the illustrations on pages 13 and 64, and colour plate 15.

Until the middle of the seventeenth century laces also meant narrow braids woven on a loom—as in the 'admiral's lace' meaning the bands indicating rank on an admiral's sleeve.

Venice, Milan and Genoa were centres in the manufacture of both gold lace and the necessary gold threads until the seventeenth century. In Spain much of the gold lace had been made by Jews, so when they were forced out in 1492 the Spanish gentlemen, who did not like being deprived of their lace, bought their supplies from Italy.

Sumptuary laws in various countries were passed at various times, usually to try to quell extravagance, but one such law in Venice in 1542: 'forbade any citizen to wear metal lace more than 5 cm (2 in) wide in case he should injure himself'. Alice Mary Bullock quotes this detail.

9. Jewellery

Instructions for making jewellery using metal threads are the same as for making a cradle for jewels or found objects in Method 2 under 'Jewels' in chapter 12. 'Creating Texture with Stitches'.

After fixing the object into the cradle and decorating it, cover the back with a layer of felt cut to fit. Glue it in place. Again cover the back with a layer of fine leather cut to shape. Oversew around the edges and then cover the stitches with chips tucking them into those already on the front of the cradle.

If it is a brooch you are making, a safety pin of some kind should be sewn to the felt backing, and then a slit in the leather backing should allow it to protrude. In this case glue the leather to the felt around the slit.

I think pendants are more satisfactory than brooches because there is less handling of the purls on the edge and so less wear. A pendant needs a loop for a neck chain or a cord. (Jewellery appears in colour plate 16.)

10. Dressing a Frame

Metal thread embroidery is most easily worked on a frame. The fabric should be tightly stretched and this must be done carefully. Once a satisfactory method becomes a habit a worker appreciates how much easier it is and how few problems develop.

For preference use a slate frame where the rollers can be tightened at will. Different sized pieces of work require frames of different sizes. Obviously a large altar frontal cannot be worked on a small frame.

If the frame is not assembled when purchased, insert the rollers into the slots of the end pieces. These may need to be rolled into the slot. Tighten the wing nuts to hold the pieces together.

Mark the centre of the tapes on the rollers permanently.

It is necessary to have a strong supporting backing material. The usual material for backing is strong, washed calico. Cut or tear a piece which is wider than the measurement of the frame width—at least 10 cm (4 in), and not longer than the measurement of the length of the frame.

Tack a hem along each end, then thread a piece of coarse string through the hem. The string supports the edge of the fabric and helps to prevent it from tearing when laced to the frame; it is not used to tie to anything and so does not need to be much longer than the end of the fabric.

Turn a hem—1 cm (½ in) is sufficient, along the sides of the calico. Mark the centre point on each side of the calico.

Match the centre point of the webbing and the calico on one side of the frame. Pin it in place at close intervals. Keep both edges smooth and flat. Repeat this step on the other side of the frame. Oversew tape to calico.

Release the tension on the wing nuts and roll any surplus calico onto the rollers so that the fabric is centred in the frame and smoothly taut. Tighten the wing nuts firmly.

With lightweight string or heavy cotton thread, lace into the calico and over the ends of the frame. Make sure that the lacing thread passes inside the strengthening string so that the tension is against the string and not against the edge of the material. The length of the fabric must allow room for the calico to be stretched within the length of the frame. The background material of your embroidery must be smaller than the calico.

It is now time to set your background material on to the backing. Mark the centres vertically and horizontally on both materials. Tack these lines so that they may be removed when no longer needed. This is an important step as any distortion of either material at this stage cannot be removed later.

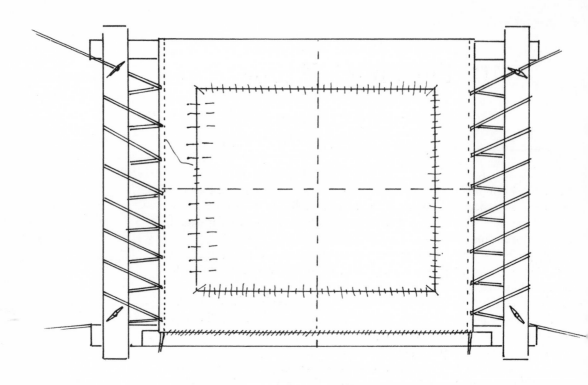

Diagram 4: Frame for working metal thread embroidery.

Match the lines on both pieces of fabric, and with very fine pins or No. 10 sewing needles, pin along these centre lines.

Working outwards from the centre, first to one corner and then to the other, pin the materials together.

Commence with the side nearest to you. Lift the upper material with a pin—the pin point should be about 1 cm (½ in) from the edge of the material. Pull the material ever so slightly towards you and towards the corner. Insert the pin so that the point is turned away from you.

When the whole side has been pinned in this way turn the frame to the opposite side and repeat the pinning and minute amount of stretching.

Repeat this on the remaining two sides. There should be no wrinkles or strained points on the surface of the material. Turn the frame over. If there are signs of bagginess on the back the calico was not stretched sufficiently at the outset. There is no way of correcting this except by taking out all the pins, tightening the calico and starting all over again.

It is essential that you turn the frame so that you are always pulling the material towards you, and also it is important that you put the pins in so that the point is away from you.

Next remove the pins from the centre of the fabric. In this part of the preparation you remove the pins around the perimetre one at a time and put a stitch in its place. As in the pinning, start the stitching in the centre and work outwards. Make your stitches in two different lengths so that any tension on the fabric will not be on the same crossways thread all the time. This is particularly important with some silk fabrics.

Bring your needle up through the background calico and put it down through both fabrics. A regular alternation of stitch length makes a tidy edge, e.g. ½ cm and 1 cm (¼ in and ½ in).

The last step in this process of dressing your frame is to tighten the rollers to stretch the fabric as tightly as possible, and to tighten it lengthwise by adjusting the lacings.

A well-dressed frame is a joy to work on.

11. Transferring a Design

1. Prick and pounce

This is the age-old way of transferring a design from paper to material.
1. Draw the design on paper.
2. Trace the outlines of the design onto tracing paper.
3. With a pricker (a darning needle stuck into a cork is comfortable to hold) make holes along these lines at frequent intervals.
4. Pin the pricked paper onto your material. Small weights, such as lead fishing sinkers, will help to keep everything in place.
5. The 'pounce' or powder which you will use to rub through the holes in the paper must be a colour that you will be able to see on your fabric. Powdered charcoal and pumice powder is a good mixture. Keep the proportion of charcoal to pumice as low as possible, the charcoal can make grubby marks on light coloured fabric whereas the pumice does not work into the surface. You must also be guided by the colour of the fabric, e.g. on a black material you would use only pumice; on a light grey material you would need more charcoal.

With a small pad of soft blanket or felt dipped in the powder, firmly press the powder through the holes in the paper.
6. When all the lines are completed take out the pins, remove the weights, and carefully lift the paper off. There should be tiny mounds of powder outlining the design. Do not sneeze or your precious pounce may disappear.
7. With a fine paintbrush dipped in watercolour paint of a colour which shows up on the material, make fine spots or lines to make an outline by connecting the dots of pounce. Leave until the paint is dry and then shake the pounce off.

2. Outlining with stitch

In this method outline your design on tracing paper as in the method above and set in place with pins and weights.
1. With cotton of a contrasting colour to the background material tack the outlines. Small stitches on the front and larger ones on the back make it easier to lift the paper off the material.
2. Remove the pins and weights and tear or lift the paper off.

One advantage of this method is that the traced outline can be taken out or altered, if necessary, during the course of the embroidery.

3. Using templates

Sometimes firm paper templates can be cut of a whole design, or parts of it, and a tacked line can be made around the shapes.

A small piece of two-sided adhesive tape can be used on the back of the paper templates to hold them in place temporarily, but it is not recommended unless the area will be covered with fabric or stitchery later because sticky residue can collect dirt at a later date.

4. Tracing with organza

This is the method that I have adopted. I find it most satisfactory. It is similar to tracing with paper *but* the tracing is tacked to the *back* of the supporting material. The outlines are then tacked through with sewing cotton in a contrasting colour. The organza is left in place.

The advantage of this method is that after applying felt padding or extra fabric to the surface you may have hidden lines which you wish to use. You can turn your work over and re-tack them through all layers.

5. Erasable pens

Pens have come onto the market that can be used to draw on fabric, and that either disappear or can be sponged. Full instructions are supplied with the pens.

Try all these methods and choose the one which suits your needs best.

12. Creating Texture with Stitches

As soon as you start putting stitches onto fabric you create texture. It will be of varying degrees of depth depending on the nature of the stitches used and the nature of the threads used.

Let us start by examining some threads. The finest of silken threads will not alter the surface appearance of the fabric very much if a flat stitch, e.g. satin stitch, is used, but it will produce a noticeable sheen against a matt fabric. However if padding is used to raise the satin stitch it becomes more noticeable. This is because the raised area will now reflect light in more than one direction, so that light and shade and even shadows will become noticeable.

Some stitches which are simple in their basic form can be adapted, added to, or combined with other stitches, to make them more suitable for richly textured effects.

Such basic stitches as running-stitch, backstitch, stem-stitch, chain-stitch and satin-stitch become rich and glamorous with the addition of extra stitches.

For example let us start with **running-stitch**. It can become: pattern darning, double running-stitch or Holbein stitch, whipped running-stitch, or Eskimo edge.

Backstitch can become double backstitch, laced backstitch, or whipped backstitch.

Stem-stitch can become split-stitch, whipped stem-stitch, raised stem band, or Portuguese border.

Chain-stitch can become rosette chain, knotted chain, broad chain, zigzag chain, raised chain band, whipped chain-stitch, or laced chain-stitch.

Satin-stitch can become long-and-short stitch.

Buttonhole stitch can become blanket stitch, or up-and-down buttonhole stitch.

The variations go on and on.

Once you understand the general idea of altering basic stitches and adding to them there is no limit to what you can do.

As Thurle Hughes said some years ago, 'Embroidery is the work over the centuries of men and women who loved stitches and experimented with them'.

'The Shield-shaped Panel', c.1500. Courtesy Bayerischesmuseum, Munich. The background is painted and has small embroidered details. The figures in the boat are in high relief and some silver thread is couched in the ripples of water.

An interesting thing about stitches is that basically, there is not a wide variety, and they vary little from country to country. I have often wondered how much we owe to the sailors of the world who have brought gifts to wives and sweethearts from distant places, and these lonely women have then incorporated these previously unknown stitches into their own vocabularies.

Of course it is also true that what can be done with a needle and a thread is limited. Today we are experiencing a great interest in texture, but it is no more than was evinced in the stump work of the seventeenth century. This fashion died out completely to become popular again in Victorian times. Then it was a reaction to the flat canvas work known as Berlin work that had taken precedence over almost all other forms of embroidery during the nineteenth century.

It seems to me that another chapter is beginning now for flatter work using dyed and painted areas as background. This also was prevalent in the early 1800s. So really embroidery has not changed so very much. Probably the one really new aspect is the introduction of the synthetic filament threads. The sheild-shaped panel on the previous page is dated 1500!

We must not ignore the knotted stitches which, in their various forms, are very textural. French knots, Chinese knots, Dutch knots, eastern stitch, Sorbello stitch, bullion knots and spider's webs all have their place.

Needleweaving is another form of embroidery that has great textural qualities.

Most of these diverse stitches can be adapted so that they can be used in metal thread work. In some cases the main part of the stitch is made by the thread in the needle and purls added when the surface part of the stitch is being made.

Metal threads give another kind of texture. The basic simple stitches rely on the threads themselves to provide light and varying textures. Many of these simple effects are very satisfying. When the work becomes complicated and sculptured, great restraint must be exercised to make sure that the overall effect does not become brash and overwhelming—see colour plate 18.

The scope of metal thread work is only limited by the skill, the imagination and the artistic understanding of the worker.

Couching of the Threads

This is the simplest method to use when beginning to do metal thread work. Take two strands of a wrapped gold thread such as Jap. gold. Thread a needle with a fine strong yellow thread. Use a fine, short needle. Make a single knot about 2 cm (1 in) from the end. Take the needle through the fabric from the front to the back and back to the front. (As metal thread work is always done on a frame, in many cases a large one, it is not practicable to turn the frame over every time to start or finish.) With two small stitches tie the end of the thread to the material and snip the remainder of the end of the cotton. You are now ready to commence laying the gold.

The thread that you will use in your needle should be waxed by drawing it lightly across a piece of beeswax. This strengthens it and helps to keep it from tangling.

Take the needle through to the back and bring it up under the line of gold which you are guiding with your left hand. The needle should be sloping out from under the gold. Take the thread over the gold at right angles to it and place the needle down sloping it under the gold. In this way the stitch will 'hug' the gold and not protrude from it.

Couching stitches should be regularly spaced. Where a single line is to be used—as in outlining—the stitches should be ½ cm (¼ in) apart. Where successive rows will be used—as in a filling—stitches can be slightly wider as in the succeeding rows the stitches are placed so that the effect is of 'bricking'.

Diagram 5: Methods of couching around a curve and a circle.

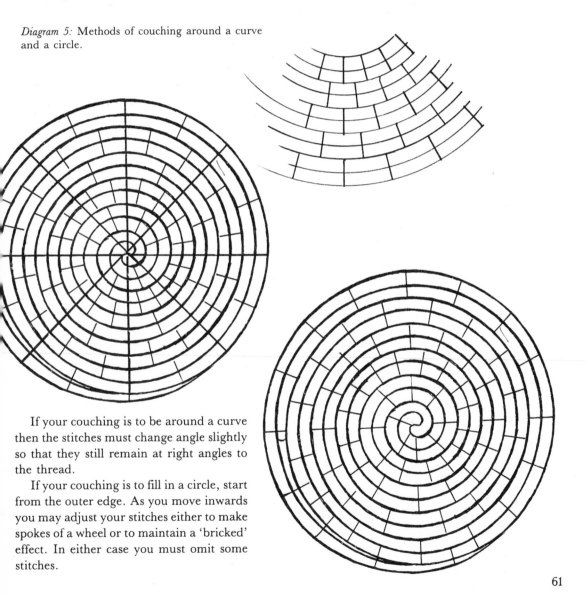

If your couching is to be around a curve then the stitches must change angle slightly so that they still remain at right angles to the thread.

If your couching is to fill in a circle, start from the outer edge. As you move inwards you may adjust your stitches either to make spokes of a wheel or to maintain a 'bricked' effect. In either case you must omit some stitches.

Underside Couching

In the metal thread work done in England up to the twelfth or thirteenth centuries, the threads were couched in a different manner. In this case the needle was brought from the back, taken across the thread, and returned to the back through the same hole. It was then given a sharp tug which pulled a tiny fold of the gold into the hole. This formed a hinge and made the material more flexible than it would be if the metal threads were flat on the surface.

This description of the method is given in every account I have read, but I wonder if it could be done from the back as in tambour beading. If the design were drawn on the back of the material, then using a short hooked needle with an eye in one end, could not the gold thread, guided by the hand under the frame, be drawn up, the needle slid through the loop, and so on to the next stitch? Underside couching does not seem to have been widely used. A modern example appears in colour plate 19.

Couching is usually done in a yellow thread, but for special effects it may be done in other colours. The closer the stitches, the denser the colour effect, as in the technique known as *or nué*, where the design in colour is painted on the background, and then the gold thread is placed across the surface and stitched in place with thread of the appropriate colour to reproduce the painted design. The entire fabric was covered in this way. There is a magnificent set of vestments made in this manner in the treasury at the Hofburg Palace in Vienna. The individual motifs would have been made separately and assembled to form the breathtaking whole (see page 38).

To finish off a couching thread, take a couple of tiny stitches on the surface of the work, and then take the thread through to the back and leave it. Tidy the back of the work later.

The ends of the gold threads which have been couched in place are cut leaving 2 cm (1 in) or so, to be taken through to the back later. By leaving them on the surface while work continues there is less chance of stitches becoming entangled with the ends.

A coarse needle is used to take the ends of gold to the back, or a sling of cotton is made in the eye of the needle and the gold placed in the sling and drawn through.

When finishing the back of a piece, the ends are either spread out and held in place with a stitch which does not show on the surface, or in some cases they can be glued in place.

Couching Cords

The embroiderer is required to roll the cord between the thumb and fingers when couching cords in place. It must be rolled in the direction which will open up the twist slightly so that the couching stitch may be placed in the groove so made. When released the grooves in the cord will close up again, and the couching thread will be completely hidden.

Couched Fillings

Some shapes are more difficult than others to fill with couching. Also thick threads are more difficult to turn at sharp corners than finer ones.

When taking two threads around a right-angled corner, work until the stitches are close to the corner, anchor the outer thread first with a stitch right in the corner (it is helpful to pull the gold thread, using the needle as a pivot, right back on itself to make a sharp fold in the thread); then place a stitch close to the corner on each side of the angle. Next anchor the inner thread making sure to keep the angle true. Then continue couching the two threads as before.

If the angle is acute it may be better to do the outer thread in the manner described above, but then take the inner thread right into the corner, cut it off leaving about 3 cm (1¼ in), and take the end through to the back. Commence the gold thread again a short distance from the corner.

Interesting textures can be created by using combinations of different threads in the pairing of threads in couched fillings. One thread of Jap. gold and one of pearled purl is a useful combination on occasions. Since there is no problem of ends fraying with pearled purl it does not need to be taken through to the back. It can be cut and stitched right at the end. Then the Jap. gold can be turned around the end of the pearled purl, and the pearled purl commenced again. The Jap. gold is turned squarely in this case and held with a stitch at each corner.

This method can be used with other threads but the end will need to be taken to the back.

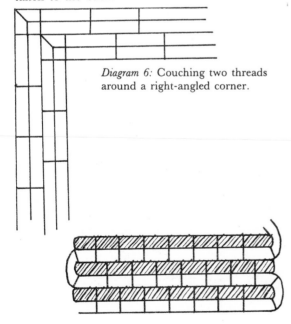

Diagram 6: Couching two threads around a right-angled corner.

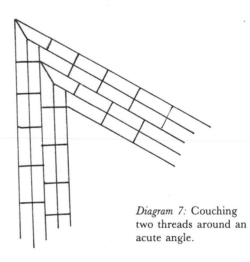

Diagram 7: Couching two threads around an acute angle.

Diagram 8: Methods of couching using one thread of Jap. gold and one thread of pearled purl.

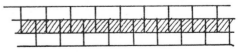

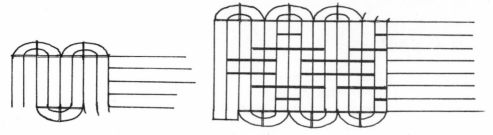

Diagram 9: Method of working borders using gold
thread to make geometric patterns over fine string.

When really crisp, sharp edges are called for, whether the filling is rows
of couching or purls, an outline of pearled purl is called for.

String can be used as padding and Jap. gold, twist, or fine plate can be
taken from side to side continuously. In the case of plate it has to be folded
on itself at every turn and should not be pressed too firmly at this stage
or it may crack. It is stitched at the edge only.

The traditional way to hold string in place is with small stab stitches which
pierce the side of the string alternately on either side. This method gives
more control over the string than simple couching. Your metal threads should
provide complete covering of the string, but it is a good idea to colour the
string yellow or grey depending on whether you are working in gold or silver.

Infant's cap, late
17th—early 18th
century, Europe.
Courtesy Fine Arts
Museum, Boston. Gift
of Philip Lehman. Silk
embroidered with silk
and silver yarns; edged
with metal lace.
Accession Number
38,1323.

Book-cover, late 17th century, Spanish. Courtesy Fine Arts Museum, Boston.
Elizabeth Day McCormick Collection. Pearls, plate and spangles on fabric.
Accession Number 43,322.

In a Russian book I was shown a method of working borders based on the same idea. Several rows of coarse thread or fine string were stitched closely in parallel lines. The gold thread was then taken from side to side. At each side it was held in place by a stitch, but using the padding threads as a guide a geometric pattern could be stitched between the parallel lines. The padding threads would indicate the relevant spot to place a stitch which could be a coloured one, if desired. This idea can be elaborated.

String is used in a number of ways as a base for metal thread work. As padding for basket-stitch, strong shapes or heavy stems, it is very satisfactory. An example appears in colour plate 21.

Basket-stitch

String padding is laid in parallel lines with gaps between the lines in preparation for basket-stitch. The width of the string should be the same as the width between the lines of string.

Jap. gold or other thread is then couched across the lines of string. The gold covers two lines of string and then is firmly tied down in the gap which follows with a stitch (two stitches on top of each other may be used, if desired); then carry the gold across two more lines of string, and tie it down in the gap. Continue in this manner until the end of the area is reached. Turn the threads around in the same manner as in ordinary couching.

On the return journey, tie the gold down so that a bricked pattern is made to create the effect of woven basketry.

Cords

Cords can be purchased for applying to designs but have their own problems. If the cord is coarse and must be taken through the material, it leaves a gaping hole which must be hidden in some way.

If it is possible to get the same effect by stitchery it may be worth the extra time taken. For instance, a cord could be simulated by doing stem-stitch in purls. There would only be the thread to finish off.

If a cord must be used, make a hole in the fabric with a stiletto or tailor's awl. Make a sling of cotton in the eye of a coarse needle. Insert the end of the cord into the sling and draw it through the hole in the fabric. Spread the ends of the cord and stitch them to the back of the fabric so that no stitches show on the front.

Using the Purls

Working with purls is a completely different technique. These fine coils are cut into the desired lengths, the needle and thread go through them, and individually they are held in place as is a bead.

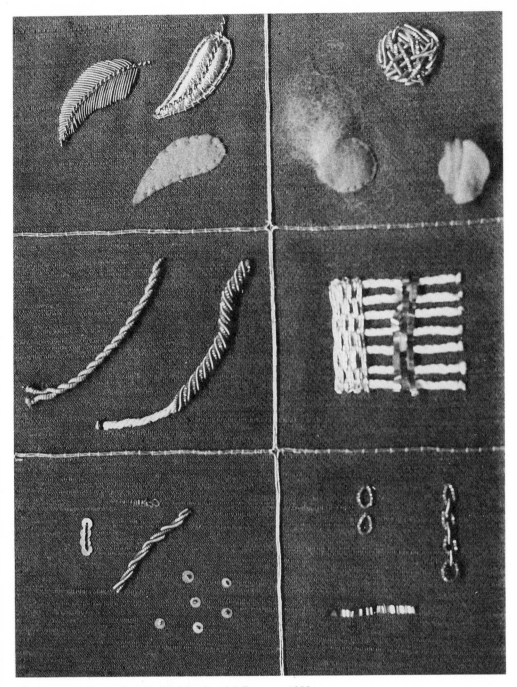

Student sampler worked by N. Morsby, Melbourne, 1988.

Top left: Leaf using purls and pearled purl. Leaf in leather outlined with Jap. gold. Leaf shape in felt.
Centre left: Laid cord. Purls laid over cord.
Lower left: Stem stitch using purls. Sewing down spangles.

Top right: Using purls. Padding with fleece. Padding using several layers of felt.
Centre right: Basket stitch using Jap. gold and using plate.
Lower right: Chain stitch using purls. Crimped plate couched with silk.

67

The length of the purls is predetermined by the design of the decoration, unless they are being used at random to fill a shape. A short, strong pair of scissors, such as nail scissors, is satisfactory for cutting. Do not use your best scissors as they will quickly become blunted.

The purls can be sprayed with lacquer to prevent tarnishing before being applied. Purls and pearled purls are most likely to tarnish. Although some threads are sold coated there is no way of telling just by looking at them.

In a shape such as a leaf, the purls should lie closely as if in satin stitch. One half of the leaf could be in smooth purl and the other in rough purl. The vein·down the middle could then be a couched line of pearled purl.

If the outside edge is beautifully smooth, it can be left without further treatment, but a couched line of Jap. gold or twist or fine pearled purl gives a wonderfully tidy finish.

It is usual to place felt padding in the shapes to be worked in purls. If only slight padding is required, one layer of gold coloured felt cut to shape will suffice. It is sewn in place with tiny stab stitches around the edge.

If the needle is slipped under the edge of the purl and the end encouraged to lie flat on the fabric, the effect is better than allowing the hollow end to show. The needle is then withdrawn. No stitch is made.

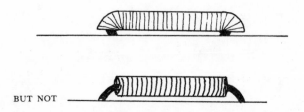

BUT NOT

Diagram 10

If more noticeable shaping is required, a small amount of fleece wool or synthetic fibre filling can be packed under the felt, or several layers of felt can be cut—each layer would be slightly smaller than the preceding layer. Loosely stitch all layers together through the centre. Tack them in position and stab-stitch around the edge of the largest layer. (The largest layer must always be on top. This will hold all the pieces in place.)

This method applies to small areas. If the area is large, each layer of felt must be sewn in place separately, starting with the smallest one.

For very sculptured effects, shapes used to be carved from blocks of felt— the type used in making saddlery.

Stem-stitch worked in purl is a lovely stitch. The individual pieces of purl should all be cut the same length.

One or more varieties of purl may be used. When using several kinds they must be used in a sequence: e.g. smooth, rough, smooth, rough; or smooth, rough, check, smooth, rough, check.

It is essential that the needle should come through the exact spot at the head of the previous stitch before making the next stitch. This is easiest to do if the needle is brought through before the previous stitch is tightened.

The length of the individual purls should allow each stitch to lie easily so that they wrap around each other slightly.

If doing a straight line, use a half-length piece to finish both ends. If doing a circle, make sure the sequence of purls will be correct when you meet up with the beginning. If in doubt work with one kind only.

Chain-stitch worked in purl is very attractive. The individual pieces must be cut in two different lengths. The smaller length is half that of the longer. The different lengths may be different varieties.

Step 1: Use one piece of the longer length and make a loop by taking the needle back through the same hole it made when it came through the fabric.
Step 2: Repeat this step making a second loop slightly below the first one.
Step 3: Bring the needle up just inside the base of the first loop and using one of the shorter pieces of purl connect the two loops. Hold the loose top one down with a bar by taking the needle down just inside the top of the second loop.

From this point you use the two lengths alternately, or you can do all the loops first and then all the bars afterwards.

Purls over String

A very strong line can be achieved by covering a line of couched string with purls.

The purls should all be of the same length. They are then sewn down diagonally over the string. It is not as easy as it sounds—the angle must remain the same as the work progresses, and the purls should appear to be wrapped around the string.

If the string goes around a curve the stitches must close up on the inner side and open out on the outer side so that the pattern appears to continue evenly. The string should not be visible between the purls.

Purls can also be massed over a felt shape. They should be placed in an irregular pattern lapping over, around and beside each other to provide interest. They may be all of one variety, or mixed, and should be close enough to cover the padded area. If greater texture is required, the shape can be made 'in the round' covered with purls on the surfaces which will be seen, and applied separately when completed.

Chequer-board Patterns

Purls can be used to make chequer-board patterns and other designs by carefully placing them in groups at various angles, as demonstrated in diagram 11. These shapes can be sprayed with lacquer to prevent tarnishing before being applied.

Pearled Purl

When purchased, pearled purl is in a coil and is very closely wound. It is much stiffer and stronger than the purls. It may be pulled out to varying

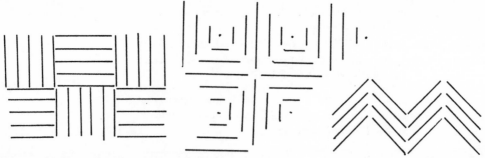

Diagram 11: Examples of patterns made by using groups of purls at different angles.

degrees of openness, but it will not return to its original form. If only slightly stretched, placing a stitch between the coils will make a click; if pulled more open the stitch will slip between the coils without making any sound. The stitches are made in the same way as for other couched threads and should not protrude. There are three sizes of pearled purl and a very fine one known as 'super X'.

When cutting chips have a cutting board at hand. A piece of heavy cardboard or plywood covered with felt or velvet, or a small supermarket tray with felt or velvet lining will help prevent the chips from jumping away as they fall from the scissors.

Working with Leather

The best leathers to use for appliqué are fine soft skins. They are not always in great supply but a good leather merchant should be able to help you. Many of the synthetic leathers are easy to handle but they come in very wide rolls and are not usually available in small quantities.

Always look at a skin carefully and mark on the back where there are any imperfections.

Also on the back mark out the shapes you wish to cut out. I like to draw or trace my shapes on to fine tissue paper, and with a glue stick put a thin smear on the leather and place the shape on it.

Cut out the shapes with a sharp knife, a razor blade or scissors. BE SURE THAT YOU HAVE NOT REVERSED YOUR DESIGN IN PLACING IT ON THE BACK OF THE SKIN. Place the pieces of leather on your work and check that they are correct.

It is helpful if you make holes in the leather appropriate to your stitching line. If the pieces are large enough you can make a line of holes with a sewing machine without thread in the needle. For small pieces this is impracticable. Make the holes with a darning needle stuck into a cork. Place a pad of paper under the leather to cushion the stabs with the needle and protect your table top.

To tack the leather pieces onto your work make stitches right across the leather—you must not make unwanted holes in leather because they cannot be removed.

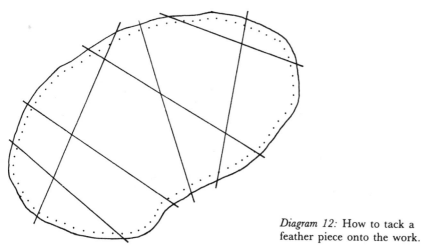

Diagram 12: How to tack a feather piece onto the work.

If this is impracticable make a tacking stitch through holes you have already punched in several places and remove these stitches as you proceed with your sewing down.

Sewing down is done with small stab stitches in a colour matching the leather. The leather should be sewn down smoothly with no bulges or pleats.

Neat, regular stitches need not be covered but if you are not satisfied with your stitching the leather appliqué may be edged with a couched thread of some kind.

Foil surfaced leathers need to be used with discretion or they tend to dominate the embroidery.

Colour plates 22 and 23 show examples of work in leather.

Spangles

This is the name given to small metal plates used from earliest times in metal thread work. They are widely used in work in the Middle East, Russia and in medieval Europe.

They can be attached by sewing with a knot of thread or a piece of purl. To attach a spangle with a purl, the needle comes up through the hole and back through the same hole after picking up the purl. Alternatively the spangle is held down by a thread which, after coming through the hole in the spangle, crosses the surface and goes back through the fabric outside the edge of the spangle. They can be overlapped to make line patterns.

Jewels

Jewels (i.e. glass stones) and found objects such as pebbles and chunky pieces of glass or shells, can be sewn onto your work, using metal threads to make settings to hold them. Here imagination is needed to make best use of the threads and the object. I have found purls very adaptable for this purpose.

To begin with, a basic cradle must be made to attach the items firmly to the material.

Method 1

Using strong paper fold it around the object until you have a collar which fits snugly. Leave the top of the object uncovered, cutting the paper away if necessary. When the fit is satisfactory it will need to be cut down one side so that the paper pattern will lie flat on the lightweight metal sheet. I used brass not much heavier than aluminium foil. Cut the metal using your paper shape as a pattern. When pinched into shape it should fit neatly around the object. Make some holes in the metal shape so that it can be tied to the fabric securely.

File the edges of the shape and the holes so that jagged bits will not cause wear on fabric or thread.

Attach this metal setting with the object inside it to the work in progress and build a decorated setting over and around it.

There are no rules as to how you use the purls, but if the pieces you want to use weave or twist are longer than 2 cm (1 in), thread your needle and cotton through the purl before you do each twist to support the coil and prevent it from stretching—see colour plate 17.

Method 2

In this method I make a cradle of detached buttonhole stitch, and then the purls can be sewn to the cradle before it is attached to the fabric.

Place the object on a piece of very strong fabric e.g. canvas or duck. Draw around the object.

Steps in making the pattern for a collar or cradle for an object so that it may be attached to fabric and ornamented with purls.

Couch a strong cotton thread in a contrasting colour onto the canvas. This couched thread should not be more than ½ cm (¼ in) inside the drawn outline. Use an ordinary sewing thread for the couching, but it is helpful if it is a different colour to the heavier thread. Finish the sewing thread off firmly.

Leave about 5 cm (2 in) on each end of the couched thread; take these ends through to the back of the material to get them out of the way, but do not shorten them.

Using a fine, firm thread make a row of buttonhole stitches through the couched thread, BUT NOT THROUGH THE FABRIC. Continue making rows of detached buttonhole stitch into the previous row until the drawn line is reached.

Finish off the thread firmly into the buttonhole fabric. No stitches must go into the supporting fabric at this stage.

Repeat this stage completely, making a duplicate piece of buttonhole fabric.

Remove both pieces of buttonhole fabric from the supporting fabric and join them around the outer edge. (It is easier to take the holding stitches out from the back of the supporting material.)

Slip the object into the cradle before the edges are sewn together all the way around.

Pull the ends of the original couched thread snugly around the object and tie them off securely. Trim the ends.

Now you can mass purls, beads or anything you wish on this firm cradle which holds the object.

Need I say that it is unwise and unnecessary to ornament the back of the cradle?

At this stage the whole item can be sprayed or painted with lacquer if desired.

When applying the finished object to your work in progress, use more purls to cover the join where the object sits on the background.

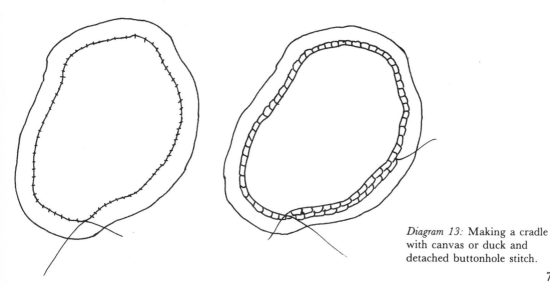

Diagram 13: Making a cradle with canvas or duck and detached buttonhole stitch.

73

Conclusion

Metal thread embroidery is still being done in many parts of the world. In this day and age items made in this technique are definitely luxuries.

There are still firms making Church, Masonic and Armed Services requirements. There are dedicated needlewomen and men who delight in producing beautiful things for their own parishes. There are groups who do civic projects to commemorate great occasions and celebrations. There are those people who experiment and try to expand the possibilities of any craft. For every success there are many disappointments.

Recently I have tried setting emboidery in clear plastic to make paperweights and jewellery. It is possible to do, and it is not expensive. It can be done in the home workshop.

If you bind pearled purl to the outside of a gold-plated ring with a coloured cotton, it gives a grooved edge into which the gold thread used to make the skeleton bars can grip. The coloured thread is removed after the design has been woven into the bars.

Embroidery done on a background of woven fabric does not give satisfactory results.

Instructions for using liquid embedding plastic come with the tin. It is available from craft and hobbies shops. I have found the slightly flexible moulds sold for the purpose more satisfactory than tins or domestic moulds, but it is not always possible to find the shape needed. Then whatever is to hand can be used.

Who knows what innovative ideas will develop along with scientific advances in the manufacture of these fascinating threads? I hope to see some of them.

Bibliography

The Orient

The Art of Oriental Embroidery, Young Y. Chung, Charles Scribner's Sons, New York, 1979.
Dragons and Other Creatures, Kay Westphal, Lancaster-Miller, Berkeley, California, 1979.
Traditional Japanese Embroidery, Iwao Saito, Shoei Shashui Seihan Co. Ltd, Japan.

India

Decoration, Designs & Craftmanship of India, Enahshi Bhamnani, D.P. Taraporevala & Sons, Bombay, 1969.
Industrial Arts of India, Sir George Birdwood, Idarah-i-Adabizali, Delhi, 1881, reprint 1974.
Indian Embroideries, Irwin & Hall, Calico Museum of Textiles, Ahmedabad, India, 1973.
Art Manufacturers of India, T.N. Mukharji, Government Printing Office, India, 1888.
Indian Art at Delhi, Sir George Watt, John Murray, London, 1904.

Hebrew

The Art of Judaic Embroidery, Ita Aber, Bell & Hyman in conjunction with Charles Scribner's Sons, New York, 1979.

Turkey and the Mediterranean

Islemeler, David Black, Oriental Carpets, London, 1978.
Embroidered Flowers from Thrace to Tartary, David Black, Oriental Carpets, London, 1981.
The Influence of Ottoman Turkish Textiles and Costume in Eastern Europe, Veronika Gervers, Royal Ontario Museum Monograph, Canada, 1982.
The Byzantine Tradition in Church Embroidery, Pauline Johnstone, London (Alec Tiranti) 1967.
Turkish Embroidery, Pauline Johnstone, Victoria & Albert Museum, London, 1985.
Turkish Embroidery, Gülseren Ramozanoglu, van Nostrand Reinhold Company, New York, 1976.
The Embroideries of North Africa, Caroline Stone, Longman's Group, Harlow, Essex, UK, 1985.
'Greek Handcraft', article by Hatjinikolaon, National Bank of Greece, 1969.

Russia and Neighbouring Areas

Gold Embroideries of Bukhara, A.I. Sidorenko, A.K. Artykova, R.R. Radjabov, Gafur & Gulyam, Literature & Art Publishing House, Tashkent, 1981.
Russian Embroidery & Lace, L. Yefimova & R. Belogorskaya, Thames & Hudson, London, 1987.
Russian Folk Arts, Alexander & Barbara Pronin, Thomas Yoseloff Ltd, London, 1975.
Estonian Folk Costumes, Melanie Kaarma & Aino Voolma, 1981.

Europe

The Art of the Embroiderer, Charles Germaine de St Aubin, 1770, translated and re-issued by Los Angeles County Museum & David Goden, Boston, USA, 1983.
Embroidery for the Church, Pat Beese, Studio Vista, London, 1975.
Needlework, an Illustrated History, Bridgeman & Drury, Paddington Press, London, 1978.
Metal Thread Embroidery, Barbara Dawson, Batsford, London, 1968.
Ecclesiastical Embroidery, Beryl Dean, Batsford, London, 1958.
Ideas for Church Embroidery, Beryl Dean, Batsford, London, 1968.
Embroidery for Church and Ceremonial, Beryl Dean, Batsford, London, 1981.
Church Embroidery, Beryl Dean, A.R. Mowbray, Oxford, UK, 1982.
Elizabethan Embroidery, George Wingfield Digby, Faber & Faber, London, 1963.
Decorative Needlework, Miss Lambert, John Murray, London, 1843.
Metal Thread Embroidery, Jane Lemon, Batsford, London, 1987.
Gold & Silver Embroidery, ed. Kit Pyman, Search Press, Essex, UK, 1987.
Couching and Decorative Laid Threads, Gloria Ramsay, Batsford, London, 1970.
The Art of the Embroiderer, Schuette & Muller Christensen, Thames & Hudson, London, 1964.
Needlework through the Ages, Symonds & Preece, Hodder & Stoughton, England, 1928.
Lace and Lacemaking, Alice May Bullock, Batsford, London, 1981.
English Domestic Embroidery, 1690–1860, Thurle Hughes, Lutterworth Press, 1961.

Museums

Museums I have visited where there are collections relevant to this topic:

Athens	The Benaki Museum
Bath	The Costume Museum
Boston	Museum of Fine Arts
Cambridge	Fitzwilliam Museum
Copenhagen	Decorative Arts Museum
	Rosenberg Palace including the Treasury
Glasgow	Birrell Collection
London	Victoria & Albert Museum
	London Museum
Lyons	Textile Museum
Istanbul	Top Kapi Palace Museum
Manchester	Platt Hall Costume Museum
Melbourne	Embroiderers' Guild
	National Gallery of Victoria
Paris	Cluny Museum
St Gall	Industrieundgewerbe Museum
Seattle	Washington University textile collection
Sydney	Embroiderers' Guild
	Powerhouse Museum
Vienna	Schartzkammer, Hofburg Palace
Zurich	Landsmuseum

Suppliers

Most well-stocked craft shops have supplies of Lurex and metallic threads.
To obtain the bullion threads it is necessary to send for it overseas.

Australia

Church Stores, 428 George St, Sydney, NSW 2000—stock Jap. gold and silver

Stephen Simpson Ltd, Avenham Road Works, Preston, Lancashire—makers of these threads. Send £2 sterling for sample card.

Mace & Nairn, 89 Crane St, Salisbury, Wiltshire, SP1 29Y—will deal in small quantities and will supply a beginner's kit.

Christine Riley, 53 Barclay St, Stonehaven, Kincardineshire, AB3 2AR, Scotland.

Needlestyle, 5 Woolmead East St, Farnham, Surrey.

Distinctive Trimmings, 17 Kensington Church St, London, W8 LF

United States

Tinsel Trading Co., 47 West 38th St, New York.

Index